A division of LUMMOX Press

THE BRENTWOOD ANTHOLOGY

by PITTSBURGH POETRY EXCHANGE

* * *

Edited by Judith R. Robinson and Michael Wurster

For Helen Faye, with admiration and love, Judy 11/17/14

ISBN 978-1-929878-57-4

First edition

A division of LUMMOX Press
PO Box 5301
San Pedro, CA 90733
www.lummoxpress.com/lc/

Printed in the United States of America

Acknowledgments for The Brentwood Anthology

Michael Albright
In the Hall of Dead Birds and Viking Tools – *Tar River Poetry;* In Name Of – *Loyalhanna Review;* The Sack of Ithaca – *East Coast Literary Review*; Gurney – *Uppagus*

Joan E. Bauer
New York Skyline, 1907- *Transnational Literature;* Duckweed- *5 AM;* Where Glaciers Scraped the Land- *Iodine Poetry Journal;* I Pretend My Mother Is Not Dead – *US 1 Worksheets;* Bithday In Bejing – *Voices from the Attic;* The Experimental Plane – *US 1 Worksheets;* Blind Date-"The Almost Sound of Drowning," *Main Street Rag, 2008* and *Prism International (2007 Earl Birney Poetry Prize)* and *Pittsburgh City Paper;* Prayer Beads & Stone – *5 AM*

Jennifer Jackson Berry
I'm Showing – *Mead: The Magazine of Literature and Libations ;* I'm Telling – *Uppagus*

Ziggy Edwards
Grandpa Remembers Electricity – Hope's White Shoes" *Pittsburgh Poetry Exchange, 2006;* The Girlfriend Machine – *5 AM*

Timons Esaias
Lines Written to an Unknown Audience Waiting for the Night's First Act—"The Influence of Pigeons on Architecture," *Yellow Pepper Press, 2004* and "Along These Rivers" *Quadrant, 2008*; de angeli – *5 AM;* Commandments for July, Willard and Maple, Thatchwork; Photonic Relationships Terra Incognita and "2001: A Science Fiction Poetry Anthology" *Aramnesis Press, 2001*; Red Beans, Rice – "The Influence of Pigeons On Architecture," *Yellow Pepper Press, 2004*

Contents

Contents *(continued)*

Contents *(continued)*

Introduction

Pittsburgh Poetry Exchange was founded in 1974 by five of us—Dieter Weslowski, Lloyd Johnson, Vic Coccimiglio, J. W. Jansen, and myself—as a voluntary association of local poets. Its purpose was to provide services to local poets, especially those outside the "university loop." We offered workshops, produced readings and events, and created a network for information.

The core component of PPE has probably always been the open poetry workshop held the first Monday of each month. Initially, it was conducted at Lion Walk Performing Arts Center. Over the years, as circumstances changed, we occupied a number of venues, including The Famous Rider Cultural Center, a conference room in the Joyce Building, and City Books. Since 2011, we have been comfortably ensconced at the Brentwood Public Library.

Despite the fact that workshop members represent varying degrees of poetic expertise, we operate as equals. It's a great place for poets from novice to master to get helpful comments and feedback on their work. In the last 40 years, dozens (hundreds?) of poets have passed through the workshop.

Among those who became nationally known would be Joan E. Bauer, Mike James, Joseph Karasek, Joy Katz, and Arlene Weiner.

An open workshop necessarily produces poems ranging from great to awful, but there has developed an agreement that the general level of poems has never been higher than now. This was acknowledged by Gene Hirsch a few months ago when he suggested we should publish an anthology.

This, dear reader, is what you hold in your hands. Pittsburgh Poetry Exchange Brentwood is not a historical anthology, but a collection of poems from the workshop now, its current members. We hope you enjoy it as much as Judy Robinson and I enjoyed putting it together.

—*Michael Wurster*

Beginning Calculus

When she was five—when she was four,
she had the numbers, wrote them out,
fifteen, sixteen digits wide,
over and over, the same order.
That was when her mother knew.

Now, the numbers weigh her down,
dragging her beneath the waves,
the false equation of common life.
Her flimsy computations won't
add up to more than chaos.

So, she runs beneath the icy stars,
pierced by night's infinitude.
She tries the number she thinks
will save her, but the line's been
disconnected, the mothership
already sailed.
                    She looks to the sky,
and starts to count:
one, seven, eight, four, two, six, nine, five,
four, three, two, one, one, one, one…

—*Michael Albright*

In the Hall of Dead Birds and Viking Tools

Micah likes dinosaurs, but they look scary
　　　　when seen up close, their bones, or whatever
has replaced their bones, assembled in full
　　　　cretaceous size. I wonder how we know
they're put back right? My grandson has no doubts.

T. rex stands erect, huge teeth and tiny arms,
　　　　big enough to swallow a little boy,
if not a whole jeep in that stupid film,
　　　　where a mosquito encased in amber
claims extinction might not be forever.

At lunch Micah pretends to eat chicken,
　　　　says, *If I got eaten by a T. rex,*
I would be dead for the rest of my life!
　　　　We sweep away the uneaten food, then
up to the Egypt Room to see mummies.

Later, he plays on my living room rug
　　　　safe from predators, prehistoric and real,
but not imagined. My daughter talks about
　　　　the cute and the dark. *He's been like this*
since Nana died, always asking questions.

He told me when Mommy and Daddy die,
　　　　he wants to, too—he'll grow out of this, right?
I can see my mother in his pink face.
　　　　No, I say, *he won't*, as the microwave peals,
and the pang of popcorn fills the room.

—*Michael Albright*

Sea Change

There was a day when I could walk
three flights, do it more than once a day.
The concierge let us linger in that garret
because we didn't speak the language
and she thought we were in love.
     We passed the winter in abeyance,
overlooking cobblestone, shadowed by July.
We'd have claret on the terrace after dark,
and toss remnants of the day's transactions,
our change raining down the avenue,
an arpeggio of copper and steel on brick.
All that mattered was for nothing to matter.

Now confined in equal ice, there is time
to tend our frigid plots, for penitence and frost.
My life, and yours, will surely end, but—
remember, we slipped into that port,
we cheated, and for then, we won.
     What I would sell, who I'd betray,
to be back again, unfettered, brave, taking
coffee on the ledge, the drowsy town nudged
back to life, fruitstands, newscarts setting up,
schoolgirls in screaming pinafores—
     seabirds resting on every roof—
waiting for the tower clock to crack
the hour, traffic to slide to a breathless halt,
as the gray gendarme bends into the square
to pick up our pennies from the street.

—*Michael Albright*

3

In Name Of

Mass General,
that shining citadel,
a dozen discrete buildings
bringing forth the illusion
of being one.

I learned every inch of it,
its footprint, at least.
I could walk from the Liberty
to the SICU, five buildings away,
barely going outside.

After the second day,
she never really came back.
Waiting, walking, waiting,
pacing the corridors,
looking for a window
that would never be open.

The day before I let her go,
I stumbled into the chapel,
feeling like a trespasser,
reading entries in the guestbook:

KH – My husband John
physicians treat, God cures
I believe

GRD – O Lord God I pray
that my wife will conceive
and have a normal baby
in name of Jesus Christ

And then, in the next box,
a blinking yellow light,
Help me,
with the initials written in,
then inked completely out.

—*Michael Albright*

The Sack of Ithaca

1.

My dad used to like to chase fires.
When we heard the alarms,
off we sailed to find the source.
Once we pulled up in time to see
someone's home in full blaze,
screaming children spread out
across the lush Florida lawn.
Now you'd never get that close,
but this was long ago, before
everything was safe, and under control.

2.

Another time we followed the siren's song,
to a block away from our first house,
our first house *here*, when I was two,
but still remembered when I was ten,
so vivid, so pink that little house was,
where I nearly drowned in a wading pool,
my dad backed over my new red trike,
and that teenage sitter, my god, my god,
I still can't say what she did to me.
I can still remember it now, or, I remember
remembering the memory of it.

3.

A thin strip of asphalt was all that separated
those square moss-dappled bungalows from
the scrub brush pine barren now involved.
Having not yet seen the news of napalm,
I had never known treetops in flame,
and while the fire burned so wild and hot,
I could only think of the ancestral home,
the bike, the pool, the young girl's skin,
how for eight years all I had thought about
was the chance of seeing it once again.
Now would I watch it all just burn?

4.

The trucks were hosing down the road
so the policeman asked us to move on,
but not before we watched a line of men
with tanks on backs and masks on faces
spraying flame, cheating the fire of its fuel,
creating a path it could not cross.
See that, son? They're creating a backfire.
That's what's called "fighting fire with fire."
But, it's all ancient history now,
back when I could still be amazed
by all the things he seemed to know.

—*Michael Albright*

Gurney

At the Monroeville Cancer Center,
no urgency, no sirens howling
as the ambulances come and go,
just the ferrying of passengers,
routine and unremarkable.

Her ashen face as they wheel her out
is amazed, afraid, and disarranged,
confused to how she's gotten there,
in front of sliding plate glass doors,
watching as they open and close.

I wonder where my mother is,
and why she's left me here alone?
Who's that old lady lying in bed,
and where does she go when
she disappears and reappears,
and disappears again?

—*Michael Albright*

New York Skyline, 1907
After *Wall Street Ferry Slip* by Colin Campbell Cooper

The artist didn't use photographs.
He stood and painted what he saw:

a pink iridescent sky & skyscrapers rising
behind old waterfront brownstones.

The Singer building and the Flatiron.
Industrial smoke fading into cumulus clouds.

In the painting, the ferry boat carries a throng
of passengers crossing the Hudson.

My husband's mother and father, newly arrived
from Poland, are on that ferry.

You can almost see their faces.
Battery on one side, Bronx on the other.

—*Joan E. Bauer*

Duckweed

In Branchville, New Jersey, home of Bear Swamp,
I'm with my new guy-friend & to prove I'm no stranger
to frugality, I find a $57-a-night special
with a bathroom painted Easter Bunny green
& a chair that wobbles on funny rollers. We're lucky.
We both can sleep through rumbly back-road noise,
brought knapsacks full of books.
I think: *My friend grew up in a place like this*
(so different from LA). He hiked, fished & scouted,
while I read & wheezed & lip-synched
Barbra Streisand. *Did he really go ice-fishing?*
What was it like, having brothers?

The August heat has morphed the daisies
—or are they black-eyed Susans—
into a thousand drooping yellow teepees. I'm learning
what grows on backwater ponds & streams.
It's worth half-wrecking the tires,
driving down this gravel road to find
the smallest flowers in the world.
What shelters bluegills & bullfrogs,
what carries more protein than even soybeans.
What we find to sustain ourselves:
double leaves, single root, air pockets
so buoyant that the tiny flowers just float-

—*Joan E. Bauer*

Where Glaciers Scraped the Land

Once there was a sea of grass—a thousand miles wide
   coneflowers cottonwoods willows

You can still glimpse: tadpole garter snake dragonfly

I'm visiting the Minnesota river-town
  my friend sprang from
    forty years ago.

*

You can get in trouble in Minnesota, you can get half-crazed
  with how the prairie never seems to end.

The way the glaciers scraped the land
 makes it hard
   for anything to root.

*

Today we're in Duluth, a shabby Great Lakes port
my friend shipped out from
  when he worked the iron-ore freighters.

I study the dead birches empty-armed, aslant.

He says: *Nothing I want to memorialize here.*

We joke about log cabins and chain-saw art
  then walk,
heads down, into the wind

—*Joan E. Bauer*

11

I Pretend My Mother Is Not Dead

but is bartering at a West LA farmer's market,
her battered shopping cart bulging with her own
purple figs, rock-hard guavas, juicy-ripe persimmons.

Perhaps she will trade them for fresh brown eggs
or shiny eggplant. Or chocolate she'll store in the freezer
because *out of sight is out of mind.*

My mother is buried at Holy Cross with the Catholic
movie stars. She herself never met anyone famous unless
you count Colonel John Stapp, the rocket-sled man.

Mother liked my poems, so long as I said nothing bad
about NASA or Charles Lindbergh or my father.
But I can't forget the double martinis my father needed

to have lunch—with me—at Nixon's favorite Mexican
restaurant, El Adobe. Dad's wife would share how
sorry she felt for 'the little people.'   She was related

to an early California governor. Maybe that's what
gave her airs. She'd been Dad's secretary.
She loved him & would bring him, without question,

the vodka/orange juice from the stainless Frigidaire.
I'd drive home repeating a kind of mantra.
You are not your parents. You are not—

Lucky: the fire in '91 spared all the family photos.
That winter, I wiped away every smudge to see
my parents smiling & foolish & young again.

—Joan E. Bauer

13

Birthday in Beijing

April thunderclouds in battleship formation
but the rain is light as we touch down.
At last, the swarming, noisy, candy-

colored streets of the city. Breakfast:
soy boiled eggs, red beans, dumplings,
strong coffee—four cups. For jet lag.

Tiananmen? Closed for 'renovation'
& no one is surprised. So our guide Mr. Ho
distracts us, talking about love, Beijing-style,

how young people pay $11 for a broadcast ad,
while old-timers ballroom dance in the park.
There are still arranged marriages. A groom

doesn't see the bride until the veil is lifted.
He tells us: *In China it's not rude to ask
personal questions, even of strangers.*

That day Mr. Ho, our host, tells us what features
Chinese men most admire in women: *oval face*
dimples small mouth straight nose

That day, my companion is cranky.
I forget something in my room & again
I don't hear (or remember) what he's saying.

I give up! There must be something
neurologically wrong with you—
that you don't hear me.

That day, Mr. Ho explains astrological signs.
He asks ours. We tell him & he laughs,
Not the best match. Sorry—

—Joan E. Bauer

15

The Experimental Plane

In Alamogordo, I trudged through sandstorms
with a bloody nose, but hid behind the kitchen door

when test pilot Roger Croman showed up drunk.
My dad would coax and reassure him

the experimental plane was solid,
that he (and it) wouldn't fall, in flames, to Earth.

My dad's gone and I think about gravity a lot:
How scientists can (and can't) explain what it really is.

Once my dad took me on a ferris wheel, and together
we looked down at my mother, a tiny figure

on the ground, screaming. Dad said something like:
She gets dizzy drinking from a tall glass.

Once we all remembered July 20, 1969.
We studied the "geometry of space."

Gravitational force= (G * ml *m2) / (d2)
(Don't ask me to explain it)

I do have a beer-mug kind of trophy on my desk:
Manned Lunar Landing Hal Bauer A3 Mission Control

What if the first particles hadn't clumped together?
A lifeless universe?

My dad would say (in his best Walter Cronkite):
Funny you should ask—

But what if there'd been no gravity?

—*Joan E. Bauer*

17

Blind Date

I drive all the way to Baltimore
for a blind date with a Chekhov scholar.

The tremor in his hands,
the way his sugar rises as he eats
three carrots. His soft-yolk eyes
dancing helplessly.

In the ladies' room,
blink at the uncertain woman
in the mirror, wonder

> *If you're free to do whatever you want,*
> *why are you doing this?*

Back with the diabetic Russian,
distract myself thinking how
sometimes in life (as in Chekhov)
nothing happens.

Then wonder, what's this poor guy thinking
and whom might I remind him of—

    Madame Ranevsky,
    the profligate widow.
    Varya, almost a nun.
        Anya the idealist,
    soul-starved, grasping whatever poison
        is pushed her way—

All of them at once?

Just then he stops pushing carrots
around his plate, says to me:

    In Chekhov, the pain is unbearable.

—*Joan E. Bauer*

Prayer Beads & Stone

I dress in black, with my old prayer beads,
a talisman for the cemetery road.

As I clear the crumpled leaves,
a stubborn November sun warms my shoulders.

Then a voice says   *go easy*
Or it could be   *ghost easy*

As is the custom, I leave a stone.

*

A friend brought me *matryoshkas*
from Moscow, each smaller

& smaller, nested dolls carved from wood,
then painted, each a peasant girl

with a green cloak & black-lashed eyes
so closely set—they nearly cross.

By the fourth doll,
there are no lashes, by the fifth, a mouse face
with insect eyes.

*

Some days I imagine our unborn daughter.
Black straight hair. Long lashes.

Perhaps a stubborn & turbulent nature,
someone who would scorn us

as we grew old. Or someone good
at chess-openings but who never understands

how to finish the game.

I imagine her crying, asking
Why does this hurt so—

I imagine our answer: *We don't know.*

—*Joan E. Bauer*

Sleepers

After the fire, we wanted comedy,
for some crazy reason: Woody in *Sleeper*
as the hapless nerd, frozen (in aluminum foil)
to awaken in 2173: the silver-headed robot,
the Orgasmatron, all the loopy sight gags.
Night after night, we'd laugh, then lie awake
listening to the midnight trains rattling:
engine, box cars, hoppers.
Years later, roaming
the net I find, for upscale paranoids: a 'sleeper
security bed' *the ultimate in protection from
hurricane, tornado, flood & bio-chem attack*
Bed as safe-room: metal re-enforced, with CD,
microwave, short wave—think I made this up?

Fish called *sleepers, four-eyed, stripe-cheeked,
duck-billed,* recede into the burrows & crevices
& coral reefs or simply die because they have no—
What is a pelvic sucker?
Maybe the whole country

should go ice fishing—hunker down in *sleepers*
look for pike & muskie & jumbo perch. Not that
we want the fish—
but solitude,
no phone, no pager.
Propane & poles & a chance to wear heavy coats
& funny fur hats. Long ago building wooden bridges
took strong supporting beams, transverse planks.
Sleepers: *strong timber,* like the sleepers of a ship,
the valley rafters of a roof—
what's unseen, yet holds.

They call Africa the 'sleeping' continent & why
shouldn't they be sleeping: refuge from war & hunger
& disease, yet the folks in Chad, Uganda, even Kenya
will tell you—they're heading toward a better world.
We 're like that, aren't we—
wanting to believe.
Even if we're just the framing timber:
sleepers on the rails.

—*Joan E. Bauer*

23

Fat Girl Rides the Bus

The seat next to me is a seat of last resort.
If I'm on the bus before you, I think:
I'm not going to worry. Life's too short.

I'm already against the window, body contorted.
If I'm on the bus before you, you think:
The seat next to you is a seat of last resort.

Did you buy two tickets? Then through your nose: *snort.*
If we're in the seat together, I think:
I'm not going to worry; the bus ride is short.

You chose to sit here! is my ready retort.
If we're in the seat together, you think:
This, this seat next to you—my last resort.

I wait for empty buses, transfer even though it costs more.
I like touching your leg. Is that what you think?
I'm trying not to worry. At least neither of us is in shorts.

Can you imagine how defensive I am at the airport?
I could use a drink.
The seat next to me is a seat of last resort.
I do worry. And damn if my life isn't short.

—*Jennifer Jackson Berry*

I'm Telling

I have new bruises now:
on the back of my hand, blue
and small as forget-me-not petals
where the medic tried
to start a line en route
to the ER, on the inside
of my elbow at the IV site
for fluids since I was losing
so much blood.
The medic told me how his wife
miscarried twice before
they had their daughter.
He gently pushed my ring aside
so he could lay his hand flat
across the top of mine
as he tried to find the vein.
He failed & I didn't get a line
until after the ER exam,
the plastic speculum clicking
into place, the collection
of blood into a white cup.
When I offered to take off
my ring, he said that man
of mine better not find out
how easily I remove it.
I feel like I've let go
of too many things too easily.
I tried to keep you, baby, I failed.
These bruises will soon fade too.

—*Jennifer Jackson Berry*

Body of Betrayals

Oh missed orgasms & inopportune menses!
Oh lack of athleticism! Oh sweat that trickles
from armpit to waistband &
strange wet spots on my sides!

I don't care so much about peeing a little
while laughing or sneezing or coughing;
the fact that I should Kegel is on me.
I'm over the curly hair. I even forgive the years

to perfect the ratio of gel to spray gel.
I'm almost ok with the machine gun string of farts
during the President's Physical Fitness sit-up test in 4th grade.
The boob pimples when you know

low cut shirts are the fat girl's only ace in the hole, just cruel.
Oh lack of lubrication when I'm drunk!
Oh mole hair on my chin! Oh hereditarily weak ankles!
Oh fall in the bowling alley, oh fall in the snow,

oh fall with jeans ripped from crotch to toe!
I'll spend the next however-many years situating myself
in my bra so my nipples align correctly.
I'll forget the embarrassment of the bloody nose

at the dive bar where every other bloody nose
it had ever seen was from blow. I'll learn to laugh
graciously when my only season of softball is brought up.
Oh trip over first base! Over my own feet in right field!

I'll do these things if you manage a good score.
Oh follicle stimulation! Oh luteinizing hormone!

—*Jennifer Jackson Berry*

I'm Showing

I've had this belly for years, this belly now
speckled with insulin shot sites, some

in varying stages of bruise. I'm four weeks
& high glucose in the mornings. I'm five weeks

& internal ultrasound wand, the first condom
inside me in over a year. I'm six weeks

& craving spicy, hot sauce splashed
on every plate. I'm seven weeks

& you're the size of a blueberry, baby.
I'm high risk, at risk of callusing every fingertip

from up to seven tests a day. Fasting,
one hour after eating, bedtime.

We are careful to speak in ifs:
if all goes well at the next appointment,

if I'm able to carry to term.
But we've told everyone too

soon. I was on incompatible meds.
I stood at my mother's fridge before Sunday dinner

four weeks ago & ate pinched fingers full of blue cheese.
The journal I'm keeping isn't littered

with cravings of ice cream & pickles, isn't
interspersed with pictures of my belly with a placard

of the time frame held to the side.
When you start a pregnancy obese, your belly

isn't for show. What I'll share with you
is a log of glucose readings & carbs per meal.

I hope my fingertips heal. I want to save you,
but I'm afraid I'm carrying you like a bruise,

that you're soon to fade, but not before you turn
a sick yellow. Not before you leave me tender.

—*Jennifer Jackson Berry*

Grandpa Remembers Electricity

August, 2003: Mama led me
by the tough udder of her index finger
down Delancey Street, speaking through her teeth
when I wouldn't stop bawling.

Vendor at one of those carts
they used to have
handed out free cups of ice cream.
You should've tasted this stuff:
crystal cold pom-poms
dripping sweet soup down your throat.

Three pregnant women sitting by a fountain
frizzed smiles at me, fanned themselves with pamphlets.
Police on bicycles leaned and chatted
on an old man's front stoop. Business people
half cyberized with sunglasses
knifed past us, dark jackets over their arms.

I remember hearing one say
This is just a taste of what's to come
if they don't fix these grids,
and hope's green garlic shoot
sprigged open in my chest
as we joined the crowd
walking across the bridge in the heat.

—Ziggy Edwards

Girlfriend Machine

Pissed at myself when I'm always touching you
first, and you don't fall asleep pressing my hand
to your chest. Then I have to wrap around you
from behind, wake up at three with sore shoulders.
Sucking your own tongue, you roll to your stomach,
impossible to hold. In the morning you
joke that I don't need my own side of the bed.
You joke about it every night. So content
because you have me (the way I wanted you
to feel) that you smile at the wall and drift off
right away. I contort. Cold, choked, and so pissed
because I was born for this. I should have more
of my own space, but never enjoyed sleeping
alone. It will be my fault when you peel off
these clinging arms, draw a line down the middle,
force me to become something else in the dark.
Self-contained unit, or broken piece of junk.

—*Ziggy Edwards*

31

A Child's Riches

I met a child on the road.
We walked together
in our muddy clothes.

In his light voice
he asked travelers for money.
Refugees and thieves
pulled coins from their sleeves.

He spent them all
on a room with two pallets,
and I kept silent.

The child led me along the warped porch
pulling my arm, but soon ran ahead.
Later I'd find him
asleep in the dirt.

In full dark I stepped from under the eaves
into a sky flooded with pinwheeling stars.

—*Ziggy Edwards*

Apartment 2F

Claire pulls on clean underwear,
preparing for her date with death.
All dressed up but steps are murder,
conspiring with gravity and weight.

Five blocks to the supermarket, five shots
for a barreling produce truck
and more piano anvil opportunities
than mosquitoes, than meteors.

Gods from their wicker-chair porch play
every endgame, outdoing each other.
They poke the crystal bubble 'til Claire inside
hears laughter in distant thunder.

She speed-walks home, double-bags swinging:
chick peas, a plastic lemon, white cheddar,
hand soap, small flasks of milk and iced tea.
Enough for three days, or four.

Plagues and riots flurry on TV
while Claire lies preserved, disappointed
when a man laces stubby fingers in her sleep.
Pressing, he whispers, "Sorry I'm late."

—*Ziggy Edwards*

Lines Written to an Unknown Audience, Waiting for the Night's First Act

Outside the sky is lowering the lights
to fit the evening mood.
Inside the early drinks
the ones you can still taste
are in hand, as are the cigarettes.

The problem for me, writing this poem,
is that I don't know
anything about you,
where you are reading this
or hearing this.

By the time I do know, it will
be too late to adjust,
to personalize this poem;
the die cast, and tonight's acts
behind us both.

It is an evening for embracing
the little deaths: the drinks,
the cigarettes, these lines,
the gap between me, at this table,
already in your past, and you.

—Timons Esaias

On Visiting the Dying Suburban Mall

The bookstore, and the colleague
I came for
gone.

I think of basilicas, the Roman
shopping malls,
dead,
turned into churches.
And there is a church, here,
moved into one
of the empty
slots.

Why am I always turning to Rome
and Greece
for comfort
and answers?
They killed their best
for being best.
Their bookstores are all closed
too.

If you build it,
they will eventually
forget why.

—*Timons Esaias*

de angeli

Reading Aquinas
on angels
one sees he was
really defining photons.

Creatures of pure light
outside the realm of time
weightless, in their natural state,
traveling in true straight lines,
which only inadequate perception
our limited point of view
sees as curved, or bent.

They can carry messages.
When they fall
there is perceptible impact
despite the absence
of mass.
And there is heat.
They end in heat.

Any number may visit
the head of a pin
simultaneously
but Aquinas fails to mention
that the pin might melt.

He resisted the notion
that there could be
too many true messages

That there could be
too much light.

—*Timons Esaias*

Commandments for July

It's July,
but they've rounded up
the cheerleaders
and put them in
Santa's Helper outfits.
White hooded catsuits.
Lacy, transparent, the openings
lined with alabaster fur.

They are all blonde.
They are representing
headache medicine.

I live in a culture
where young, blonde,
slender, pretty
is a résumé.
A job description.

Thou shalt not deplore it.
Thou probably ought not notice it.
There are competitions,
but, I suspect, thou shalt not
wonder when youngblondeslender
will be an Olympic sport.

Thou shalt not suggest
that Christie's handles the auction
when they go private.

Thou shalt drop the Calvinist bifocals,
my friends insist.
Youngblondeslender is a virtue,
they say, like charity,
or a wicked curveball.
Only coroners
really judge people
by what's inside.

—*Timons Esaias*

Photonic Relationships

The newspaper said that photons were entangled
And messages can now be sent faster than light.
Despite what Einstein said;
Despite what Bohr said.
But what my brother said.

I thought the article begged more questions
than it claimed to answer:
Wasn't "photon entanglement" presuming the consequent?
And how could they rule out artifacts
of measurement?
But my brother said, Don't you see the
paradox? Don't you see the answer?

So I started in with logic,
with my suspicion that quarks are only
our era's very tiny
epicycles within epicycles…

But my brother said,
Space and Time are irrelevant.
There are not two photons,
but one thing only.
Tweak it here, and it moves there,
instantaneously,
only because
it is One.
Despite what Einstein said.
Despite what the paper said.

41

We live six hundred miles apart,
The better part of an hour
at the speed of sound.
Three point two two thousandths of a second
at the speed of light.
We don't talk often,
and see each other less.
But my brother says,
Space and Time
are irrelevant.

—*Timons Esaias*

Red Beans, Rice

Today I am ignoring Pythagoras.
Don't get me wrong, he was right
about so much, about numbers, dead right,
more than almost anyone understands.
But on the subject of beans,
the necessity to avoid,
Pythagoras is best looked upon
with charity.

Today I am spending the day
with beans. One pot red beans;
the other pot a diversity,
eight varieties grown in my garden
the seventy square feet of boxed earth
parked on my city-lot driveway.
They are soaked in wine
flavored with salt pork, buried in onions,
anointed with oil,
the eight kinds and the one kind.

It's an all-day job,
an eight hour shift,
to cook them down,
snatching quarter-hours to
write this poem to you,

and a story later; quarter-hours
between stirring, though
toward the end, as in
any good alchemy,
they will require constant attention
lest the heavenly concoction burn
and be cast into the trash pit
forever.

A day, eight hours,
and then one more hour
to cool down, before they are
poured into crockery
and refrigerated.
All this time for a side dish.
Inefficient, a massive waste of
energy and time, or so it looks
on paper, and so Pythagoras might
argue, but neither assessment
penetrates the mystery, explains
why friends are heard to ask
in my hearing, if it is not perhaps
too long since
I made beans.

Religions use the metaphors
of fermentation, bread and wine, metaphors
of cooking, and then claim these
reflect underlying spiritual truths.
It is a lie.
The underlying truth is that
their analogies are stolen
from the real miracles
of the kitchen, are pious
hopes that something about us
will mirror the transformation
I will achieve today, with these
eight hours and the one,
turning simple ingredients into ambrosia,
drawing people to my table
not for a communion that is *like* communion,
but for communion that *is* communion.

Common garlic and household pepper sauce
already simmer in the formula.
In a few hours I will sprinkle in
salt, mined from the earth,
the rediscovered remnants of an ancient sea.

—*Timons Esaias*

Goodnight

I'm walking in the neighborhood.
Night sky on my eyelids.
I move the constellations around,
reposition the Big Dipper —
its proximity to Polaris.
My skin is chapped.
My veins swollen.
This isn't a commonplace event.
Old age, rocks and trees look up with me.
My mother's been dead for nine years.
I see her clearly.
She wears a string of pearls.

I'm walking in the neighborhood.
I can't say goodnight to her.
She's out on the town.
I've compressed the vastness.
She walks in this space.
I call out to her.
She answers without being there
without returning home.
She goes on living

—Mark Goldman

Sweet Lantana

Sweat runs out of me.
Every pore in my body
is awake and dripping.
Doing sit-ups on an exercise board holding
a 35 pound weight against my chest I recall
cherry lantana
I planted in front of azaleas.
Such sweet fragrance.

What a design flaw!
Such imperfect chemistry.
Much more enticing to exude
the fragrance of flowers
than repetitious sweat—
the pain of stamina.
I envy the fragrance of a blossom
bursting in the sun.

Lantana
you don't sweat
nor do you need a shave.
I walk in the garden.
A cool shower refreshes us.
We have a thirst and share an orange.
I chew a succulent piece for you.
You spit out seeds.

—*Mark Goldman*

Snowman

Right now, the snow
is too familiar.
I'm alone and cold
on a frozen field.
The hemlocks humbled,
bent low with ice.
Boughs split rough.
I'm crusted with harshness.
I mimic the unpredictability,
the instability of snowfall,
and wound you deeply.

A severing February wind
I don't understand
I don't understand
how I wound.
It's cold and getting colder.
My words freeze.
I intend to defend
and protect you
from your wounds.

I sit with you.
I begin by dressing wounds.
I search for strength
in winter, to reshape the misery.
I'm mindful now. I invent a snowman.
Snow reshaped to reassemble
a human figure
with misshaped carrots
broccoli buttons
and cranberry ears.

—*Mark Goldman*

47

New Moon

She must have wanted time to herself.
She was hiding not hidden. There's a big
difference between hiding and hidden
when you're that big!
Hiding is more trusting.

I'll show you where she lay down.
I can find the valley again.
I watched her. She didn't travel far.
I was hiking in the evening.
She took me by surprise.

Vacationers go to great expense
to watch the expanse of the moon over
Cairo or Tangiers. Not wanting to be effusive
or take up too much space,
but wanting to rest in a familiar bed,
she quickly turned out the lights
without fussing with fancy sheets.

I didn't wait for an invitation to lie down
alongside the moon. I invited myself.
I rushed home and grabbed my sleeping bag
and returned with my dog, Dudley.
He wouldn't alarm her;
he didn't bark at natural shapes.

We hid there with her. I didn't know
what I would say when she woke up.
I could ask her how it felt to be so out of place.
The moon could answer and tell me she was really
returning home again, rejoicing in the essentials
of the ordinary, when the ordinary
becomes extraordinary.
She would wake up soon, throw on the lights,
and return to an ordinary sky.

—*Mark Goldman*

49

Reaching

The sun breaks free of the clouds
draws moist air from August lawns
to cold black space

It sends streams of photons
to penetrate this frozen shell
meld fire to fire

You leave me
hot air changing
to a cool breeze

I hold tight
reach for answers in gelid vacuums

between sun and earth
between my heart and yours

—*Barry Govenor*

The Amount of Time Available

In the *Express* lane,
shoppers stand quietly, wait
as a patron fumbles for a check,
scrawls a name & amount
& finally, a signature.

~

Five-year-old Jane sits silently still
until five hours later,
the hen's egg finally drops,
then follows her addictive curiosity,
meticulously measuring chimpanzee
nuance for over a quarter century.

~

On the 61C, in Squirrel Hill,
my fellow passengers become
disgruntled, fidgety.
They shift & squirm, their body
language writing novels,
all because the Port Authority driver
won't roll the bus over a swollen fire hose.

—*Barry Govenor*

American Bald Eagle

From our canoes on the Yukon
we spot the white head

watch a powerful lift off
talons fully extended

folding wings that follow
keen eyes' focus to a steep dive

to arced claws
clutching a writhing Coho

On the ferry
while passing through the Tongass
the naturalist tells us

*The greatest concentration
of eagles in Alaska
is at the Ketchikan garbage dump*

On Pittsburgh's South Side
I *watch* pigeons
think of Ketchikan

—*Barry Govenor*

Tobacco, Birch, Cellophane

The exploding cigarette trick failed
because Mom wouldn't
allow me to load both ends
of the no filter Chesterfield.

Dad was a two pack a day man,
the fumes from the finishing mill
& the sulfurous air of his own backyard
not enough to deter him from tobacco.

Gunk not caught in his lungs
escaped as smoke
or joined the tarry waste
where, one after the other, he butted
the remnants after the last ash fell.

Each pack had a red strip of cellophane
he'd carefully tug free,
methodically grasping the end
with his long bony fingers,

the same fingers that deftly guided
tons of steel, followed hookers' directions
to set down & free red hot coils from
the crane's C-hook.

He'd put it aside 'til after supper,
finish the *Charleroi Mail*, then pull
out a birch toothpick, fiddle a while,
before gliding the cellophane
along & between his enamel.

—*Barry Govenor*

Allegheny River

Waders slosh through current,
rubber sideling cold against denim,
our faces misted in muted light.

We watch sunrise in silence,
listen to water slip around
rocks and fallen branches.

Past the last of the mist,
light, bright off the water,
pierces squinting eyes.

I look down, through
light-dappled shadows
to crayfish & minnows

then turn toward you, artist,
your cast one smooth motion,
practiced fingers one
with line and lure.

That hat, sweet pickle green,
worn visor & low crown
hugging your skull like an old friend.

Sometimes it's your pole,
sometimes mine, bent to the current,
lure snagged on rock.

Sometimes a largemouth
takes soft-shell or helgramite,
uses current as ally,
fends off the net.

In morning & evening mist,
in afternoon heat,

we stand   and wait,
wait, watch and listen.

It's the moment we catch,
more than anything.

—*Barry Govenor*

Wide World Photo 1944

A hot southern sun

        comes in handy

somewhere

        in the South Pacific

where all the conveniences of home

are not   at hand

a magnifying glass

        harnesses the magic fire

lights   my uncle's

pipe

—*Barry Govenor*

Some material for this poem from the caption of a Wide World Photo 1944, most likely from a Donora or Charleroi PA newspaper.

y 9, 1944

Sun Acts as Pipe Lighter

ng Back
es
bsidies

ton, dairy
if there

ple. It's
that you
ljustment
than $300
tis, from
ou could

the food
ts armies
ift boards
ff Butler
most valu-
ed men at

men to be
part of

t regula-
burden
n prices
still the
all the
etween
price

—Wide World Photo

A hot southern sun comes in handy 'somewhere in the South Pacific' where all the modern conveniences of home are not at hand, for, as seen here, its rays can be harnessed as emergency pipe lighter. Sergeant Charles V. Mahalic of Mount Carmel, Pa., left, employs a magnifying glass to draw the "magic" fire from Old Sol as Sergeant Miner G. Lynch of Donora, Pa., puffs away to get his stoker going. Both men are members of the Marine Corps.

county in 1943 tell the story better than any arguments or mine—or any Government statistics either. I kept track of farm sales last year. Just 135 Butler county farmers went out of business in the year, sold off equipment and stock. If there were only 10 dairy cows on each of those farms that's 1,350 dairy cows out of business in county. Of course some

"But OPA and the boys at Washington denied that increase. Instead they dipped into tax money and set up a subsidy program of 40 cents a hundred pounds on Pennsylvania production. They started paying the subsidy Philadelphia milkshed.

Deconstructing Football

The sport reduced to a verbal equation:
"the arbitrary impugning of physical motion
with numeric imperatives."
   Scoring physics/inertia is absurd.
Inertia divided by roaring crowds is absurd.
     With warface vestal virgins, "Immaculate reception,"
   "Hail Mary pass," this is secular religion at its finest.
    Why is church attendance so low?
It's because Jesus doesn't throw a ball
and the saints don't go out for a pass.
   Stadium bursting sport is kinetic, tangible (I win; you lose);
    emptypewed religion is static, intangible (I Am).
      Derrida would giggle.
Inertia divided by higher/lower numberplay equals
public drunkenness/street pissing/sidewalk brawling/
car toppling/kiosk burning.
   Even Roland Barthes would agree.
If alive, he'd probably say,
"Take your eyes back to that of a child watching this
and you'd think it was overgrown boys
playing in a giant's playpen."

—*Johnny Hartner*

58

The Body Alembic

Strange alembic, this body.
"You are what you eat,"
metaphor lost on me.
Came along "taking it all in,"
And cleaned it up somewhat.
    Taking it all in
countered with, juxtaposed by,
getting it out of your system.
not penned in latin under
some green banker's lamp in a doctor's office:
these are the verbal prescriptions,
pharmaceuticals of
well-meaning quackeries of friends, relatives,
concerned lovers.
    In times of need when the house explodes,
the girlfriend splits, the companion animal dies,
the suburban shamans make the house call
with a sympathetic arm around the shoulders:
"Take two aphorisms and call me in the morning."

59

So you take it in what wasn't meant to be;
then you get it out of your system with sex, drugs, rock 'n roll,
the usual fanfare.
Pick your poison.
Take it in and get it out; take it in and get it out.
After twenty thousand "not meant to be's,"
I'm inclined to demand what the hell is.
Strange alembic, this body and soul
where pseudo-alchemists dump and extract
such oh-so-soothing clichés like Haitian *ooma-gooma.*
Such tin expressions
Grand elixir to distill our sorrow—
presto-change-o!
the fool's gold of tomorrow.

—*Johnny Hartner*

By the First Light of Day

I see the outline of your face.
My eyes turn beyond,
to the strokes of black cedar
cast against an amber sky.

Trees bend to the water
that lies before them.
Your silver hair
wisps back
from the brim
of your forehead.

Sunlight streaks
across the lake
to glance your features,
splaying opal hues
that kindle your smile.

I follow the furrows
in your smile
beyond the first light
of day, beyond
the silhouettes of cedar,
to the irrepressible
brink of the sky.

—*Gene Hirsch*

61

Loft

We came together
in the abandoned loft.
My excitement rose,
to love someone
I could trust.

As we spoke,
she opened her sack.
She offered me a wig.
As we chatted,
she offered me a silk dress.
We quipped as she
painted my lips and
tinted my cheeks and
primped my hair.

I fell into her stockings and
shoes and she gasped
to see me rise
and strut and gaze
into her mirror, and
curtsy and smile and
bend to kiss her forehead.

I captured her exuberance
from the comer of my eye—
just as she opened her arms
to engulf the evening,
just as she gathered herself
with the passion of seeing me
happy again.

—Gene Hirsch

Were I To Rock My Hobby Horse

Were I to rock my hobby horse
up and down, were I to go nowhere
or prance into the path of a Spanish beauty—

I could give you fact
upon fact, but could not
improve upon the graceful
lines of the duchess
in her white chemise,
her red-sashed hips,
sprawled across a divan
to enhance the expression
on her simple face.

Yes, Goya was a genius!

His peasants died from want,
huddling for bread,
bending their mules
and their foreheads
to their carts,
strapped and beaten,
making haste to the altar to
purge themselves of sin.

Still, if I had no woman,
were I to ride my hobby horse

up and down through Market Square,
huddling for bread,

a Spanish goddess could sweep me
off my steed and into her bosom,
from which I'd never return.

—*Gene Hirsch*

Little Man

Men cry for lack of women.
They stand in black berets
by their windows, pipes in hand,
sullen, studying petals of snow outside.

They've missed their dinners painting
distortedly all the beauties
they could find. One need only recall
the cubists to view the misshapen
sides of their ladies' faces,
in several planes at once.
Theirs were the images that fought
to exist, that could fly
by the cryptic exaltation
of their genius.

Why do I speak to you at all?
I suppose because my face
looks up to your naked body;
my canvas filled with accolades
I've concocted for me to adore.

My words were jagged
when you first knocked.
I came to the keyhole
to find only languor,
same as mine, and I ached
to make love to your gifts.

But a new day breaks and I whisper
only, another day breaks.
My throat is shackled, fibroids
for a tongue. I can tell you nothing
of the night before,
not even where I've been,
standing nude in my black beret
by the window, painting snow.

—*Gene Hirsch*

Sign of the Cross

Tonight, I wonder
if Jesus could have imagined
that the cross of his dying
would be reinvented here
some 2,000 years later
as a small ornament
tonight's door prize
an electronic gadget
of blinking, colored lights
hanging from a necklace
on a shapely young woman.
Dancing at this nightclub
to the DJ's trendy music

she's the center of attention,
she's the young man's dream.
Red, yellow, and blue lights
moving in rhythm, in sync
with the graven image
of her plunging neckline.

Are we looking for love
while looking for a prayer?

My upbringing, my catechism
warns against violating chastity.
How lovely, the doctrine
how real, the woman.

—*Joe Kaldon*

I Covet Your Wife

sitting over there, betrothed hands
set pensively on crossed legs,
her back upright in perfect posture,
and sandy blonde hair tumbling
over a white cashmere sweater
adorned by a silver necklace
with a small cross
nestled on her bosom.

Sometimes alone,
sometimes with her mother,
with the rest of us today
she listens to the priest recall
the spoken words of Jesus
from his Sermon on the Mount:

I say to you that anyone
who so much as looks
with lust at a woman
has already committed
adultery with her in his heart.

Words today, words from antiquity
conveyed by a shopworn sound system,
as I contemplate the sinfulness
of my desire to sit one row
behind her next Sunday.

—*Joe Kaldon*

Nickel & Twist

Always tucked in a bottom drawer, the crammed Cashew Crunch tin I dragged
around since childhood with a happy face button for sad days, plastic totem pole,
joy buzzer to razz friends, a fake molar with forked bloody roots in a plastic box
labeled THIS TOOTH IS MINE—miniature charms—a horseshoe inscribed
Lucky with a gold star—and they were real, if puny and plastic, unlike stars
too far away to count—so I mapped my constellations at the A & P where it was
luck-of-the-draw-hit-or-miss with the nickel & twist machine—got Hong Kong
junk to dream on—3 Siamese cats strapped by their necks with a silver chain—like
classes, keggers and boys in college where I played Antigone in rags wound around
me & defied lots of rules but didn't die for it—I read them—U/R/OK pendant,
purple owl, blue dancing bear banging a drum—helped others read signs
which were everywhere—but the homeless mentally ill were impervious to clues,
they needed food and meds and mercy and I figured that's what we all need
(minus meds maybe) so I fed and forgave my family of origin plus the new one
I made—our shared tracings—leaping swordfish, hula girl, Pharaoh's head,
clamshell—held like discernment, in the hand.

—*Sheila Kelly*

68

The Accident

One afternoon while I was driving, singing
a dirge about mercy so sweet my heart
must have amped a little as the song peaked
in white August sun—my Honda, my blouse,
her headscarf—white, white, white—and
turning left I hit her. After I jumped from
the car, it went something like the song
and the singing—bluesy, bruising—bodies
in amber: So Sorry I Didn't See You
arced over the scene as arms slow-motioned
her to lie-down-lie-still in that spot—soon
shrill fire & rescue, shouts, cops, glares,
queries, stripped me out of Joe Henry's
God only knows to my knees on a penitent
street, wet with her gallon of spilled milk.

—*Sheila Kelly*

Tipping Point

See the Arctic—you can book a Princess cruise
      for a little whale-watching before
the glaciers, that ballroom of glistening brides, shed their veils,
before white icing runs off earth's cake

See the tundra at the edges, boreal forests beyond,
      drying their tears in ice world, uncovering treasure of carbon—
          white crinoline hoop skirt, blackening

The way strong attraction between people melts and reveals
Wherever great forces push things off kilter
      like love, thinned out over time, begins to fray

See how our friends leave one another, dropping
      off the face of their families
Forces—stronger perhaps than what drew them together,
stronger than Susie's or Jean's wedding dresses, faded,
      no longer able to reflect a mongering darkness
         behind their husbands' teeth

There's a name for the dark open water
        for the loamy pitch
            for the thawed forest
when it uncovers, when it absorbs the heat of a stranger—
        as all women and men contain bold heat

When the ice shelf cracks, and the sea
        becomes wider and deeper and blacker
see how it picks up speed when a cup of coffee becomes a kiss
        (white dresses pooling in the streets)

It's not how the Arctic should be—
        all those billions of metric tons of released need,
how rising temperatures start slow,
        build with a speed nothing can stop

—*Sheila Kelly*

Eat Your Heart Out Joie Chitwood

Joie Chitwood -1912-1988
Daredevil stunt-car driver,
racer and operator of
"Joie Chitwood Thrill Shows"

In my red coaster wagon
left knee in the bed
right foot pumping cement
pushing off at the top.

Red flyer racing
banging over the cracks
aiming straight at
the bump
in the walk
heaved high
by the roots
of the Elm
in front of
our house.

Then, airborne at last!

Bone thunked bone
when the wagon
dropped down
hard jerk on the handle
skidding through gravel
tumbling into tall grass.

—*Kathy McGregor*

1954 County Fair

Rev. Thomas got an editorial
in the Evening Gazette,
preached a hard sermon,
roused the ministerium,
wrote the County Fair Board.

In lieu of holy scripture,
Ban Hooch Shows from the Fair
went up on the notice board
anchored in the lawn of Grace
United Presbyterian Church.

Huddled talk in Barkley's
hardware, at bridge tables,
A&P checkout and Esso pumps.

The County Commissioners
debated, but declined to act.

Opening day of the fair,
junior-high daughters
of diverse congregations
took up a vigil at dusk, standing
in halter tops, shorts
and rolled-down socks,
between the cotton candy truck
and the Legion bingo game.

They stood to witness
whose fathers', promising protest,
came to picket; and whose, blessedly, did not.

Thus, accidentally, they could testify truly
that Ann's brother, blind in one eye from Korea,
purple heart pinned to his tee shirt,
did walk up the steps, pay five dollars and
disappear behind the parted curtain
to watch the hoochy-coochy girls dance.

—*Kathy McGregor*

Topography

She headed up through
the berry patch. The best way,
even holding back, pulling
loose, prickly thorn branches
to do it. Took a path through skurls
of oak and hickory leaves past
rocks heaved up out of the slopes.

Scythed through tall field grass
to the base of Reservoir Hill, toed
her boots into dirt-gravel, bent
to the slope, crabbed to the top

where wide open sky found her.

Circled the reservoir,
sat on stones,
her back against
the chain link fence
that guarded
the town's water.

Looked out on a map of small below.

White's Woods bare now.

Scratch-hatched streets.
Water, Church, Chestnut,
Elm led to school, crossing
streets with number names.

Her home, there, at the edge
where the streets quit.

All framed by fields ordered by farms.

Distant. Distinct. Quiet.
except occasional far off
yalps of cooped dogs.

She simply sat
hugging her knees,
holding herself. And,

it rose, soft eyed, like
October dawn sun
flooding out over
pouring down into
Bryce Canyon one year.

She stretched her arms wide
breathed deep, big, clear.

So much of what
mattered below
dissolved up here.

She sat for long until she thought
they'd notice her gone, so went down
trailing a stick, touching ground.

—*Kathy McGregor*

Spectacle of lights

in Christine's back yard

shrubs trees and
lightning bugs

in the ambiance of dusk

the arch of trees and greenery
encompassing the deck

we sit and watch
their flickering

—*Jolanta Konewka Minor*

River

(for River cleanup)

My eyes fill with water

gracefully flowing River—still,
through
not rocks anymore
or driftwood
but scraps of metal
abandoned
disposed of appliances
glass and plastic bottles
tires upon tires
instead of flowers
green lash grass...

the water flows—still
still beautiful
determined
though it can not
sustain life
at this
very moment...

—Jolanta Konewka Minor

79

every bit of everything

it's going to take every bit of everything to make it through everyday
the river weaves broken branches into blankets of flowers on the river bank
I keep walking under bridges
under assumptions there is no where else to go
and going forward will not get me there
just every bit of nowhere
we're all on the same bus
just different towns
the river is brown
the morning does not come
I've become the things I bury
the things I carry
the things I own
         own me

a knapsack full of souvenirs and tears
deep breaths and daydreams
it seems my backpack is my soul
and I know a million smiles could never mend the million miles between us
I run like trains
pitter-patter like rain
here and there
every bit of everywhere
sleeping on park benches
weeping at the river's edge
begging for change
begging for me to change
change every bit of everything every day

—Edward Murray

Grounded

The boy on the bus asked me why I didn't fly.

And as the Earth broke into pieces, I looked into his eyes, his pupils as big as Pluto. He still believed he could fly. My parents sewed my shadows to my shoes a long time ago and I lose myself in my shadow everyday. I won't be the one to tell him why he can't he fly, I just won't.

Me and my little brother learned to fly. We would put trash bags in our pockets and climb up on the roof through the branches of the tree in the back yard. And as the asteroids broke into pieces, the trash bag parachutes became our jetpacks. We jumped from rooftops, landed on the moon.

I used to call my little brother, "my little brother," and he would get so mad at me because he was a lot taller than me. The boy on the bus looked like "my little brother." We stopped each block at every bus stop, he asked why so many astronauts got on our rocket ship.

And as the sky was falling, I asked him his name. I said, "George, they promised us jet packs too, we all just can't afford to fly every day, we all have to work to dream." There were too many meteorite showers. I sat back powerless.

And as the world broke into pieces, I thought to myself, what it takes for the mighty to fall. The day my little brother died, I threw my jet pack in the closet back behind my old shoes and old shadows. I told ground control I was out of control. I couldn't deploy the emergency landing gear and figured I would burn up during reentry.

I took one small step after one small step for one kind man, my little brother. I sewed a new shadow to my new shoes. I hung up my space suit and hemmed up my pants. I can't tell this big-eyed little boy he can't fly. The days still hurt.

I hid behind newspapers, in the back of the bus, my soul, a black hole. I stopped walking on the moon. I folded the newspaper as I fold, neat creases, and as I broke into pieces, George asked me again, why I didn't fly.

—*Edward Murray*

new shoes

I head out the door
      and I'm not sure what I need more
      you or a new pair of shoes
fancy ones with a sun burnt brown hue
no holes in the soles
that lets the rain get in
so...
I grab my jacket out the closet
put my hands in my pockets
strut down Braddock Avenue
      and all I need is a new pair of shoes

I ain't got nothing to lose
I could have
      and should have
         loved you more
and I'm not sorry
      I just would have
            worded it differently

eventually
you reach a point when you're done
please...

I need some Hush Puppies
up jumped the boogie from the bottom
it's autumn
     and I ain't gotta sing no blues
     I'm just gonna get me a new pair of shoes
     with a little bounce to 'em too
now, I don't know what the answer is

     when we're both right
just gonna sing to the night

     and I'm done fighting
I've already done paid my dues
and I hope you get a clue
with a little bit of whiskey

     I know I'm your old pair of shoes
I got everything to lose
     and I don't need no shoes
all I need is you

—*Edward Murray*

friend

shh...
listen
can you hear them
they're coming for me
they want every part of me
and part of me wants me
to give it all to them
and even when the sky is falling
and even when regret is calling
calling you
remember me
crazy and free
I like to play the piano
       the piano, the piano
people think they play me
       play me, play me
I am a symphony
I am glass bones in a straitjacket
I am the shadow of the earth on the moon
in this white padded room
sitting in the middle of this concrete floor
looking at the slot in the metal door
they're coming for me
listen
shh...

—Edward Murray

summer

she is all that I am
all that I will ever be
she is gravity
sits like humidity
she looks down on me like moon
she is summer afternoon

we start southeast on Penn Avenue
you and I
blue skies reflect in your beautiful eyes
soft hand in hard hand
two lightning bugs in a jar
cars drive by
music blaring
people staring
you and me
we are electricity
I hold my breath
we tum left and left again, going west
downtown around Fifth
we sit like steam
melt like ice cream
summer supreme

last week
right in middle of the Grant Street
you set my heart on fire
burned down my soul
rolled me up
put me in your heart
we are now heart and soul
you hold me sweet
summer beats in the park
summer heat in the dark
you kiss me fireworks
hold me summer
sweet summer morning

oh, the melody
she, she is all that I am
and all that I will ever be
she, she is my gravity
we, we are electricity
we, we are summer

—*Edward Murray*

tiny towel

One must slip out
of one's
harmful dharma

as from an open robe
before the onsen

—Stephen Pusateri

He had a mouthful of sparrow bones

A stray, blackened feather
poked through the spacious cage
of his greasy smile
The burnt-wing smell
shifted through the stilted hut
It hovered over the spot
where animal became meat

He smoked his wisdom between ten teeth
His laugh could have cut
each bird from its flight
had they room to fly
His V-neck was only white
at the shoulders
where the river water hadn't reached
He was happy to teach me
for cigarettes and a few scraps of gwilo cash

I'd been told to push my motorcycle
the last two miles into town
so no one would steal it
thinking it busted
The morning I'm to leave
I rev the engine
The boys of the village chase me
as if running me out for the assumed lie
of the broken bike
The secret I've gleaned
is that something precious must always die

Back home in DC, I've opened
two new restaurants inside the Beltway
Each serves only baby birds
They're a hit
I'm on magazines

—*Stephen Pusateri*

At Sea Shell Island

the sky turned milky opalescent
and lost distinction from the great sea beneath it.

They shared the same pearled translucence
through which showed only a bare hint
of the shore at Sea Shell Island,

the line between sky and water, one from the other.

And somehow I thought of you,
dark edge turned to light and song,
all you meant to me.
Now lost, and closed, as these things go.

What after all is two together
in this dance of life

I only knew with you,

a calm sea, the completed sky,
all that otherwise eludes.

—*Judith R. Robinson*

No Rest

Deep within one gray
fold of memory
near the dotted
wing of owlet,
the country day
of fawn,
the orchard—
a synapse
skims   dips
but does not
summon up your body;
impossible to
assemble
parts as whole;

ironic bulges
stand apart
as does your face,
eyes, complexion,
pouty lips
that kissed too small
and talked too large
remain separate
but keep on

calling
urging
swallowing.

—*Judith R. Robinson*

Losing A Jewel

windblown hair
red lipstick   espadrilles
all eyes all limber all slender
blonde days in Rome
unclutchable as quick silver,
tears,   butter,   water,
impossible to hold
except in the deep
gray folds of memory
look there
underneath thin yellowed skin
a winking eye
the last deep russet gleam
the quick hand
skims   dips
wills it to stay
it will spill
impossible to keep
impossible to walk away.

—*Judith R. Robinson*

Pale Blue Light

She feels
a heaviness
on her chest
burdensome as
the memory
of bulky woolens
forced on her
by Mother
even as the sun
melted crystalline
snowy days
into seepage
down the Slopes
so long ago;
curious how
pale spring
light in afternoon
bears back
that weight,
that gloom,
unchanged.

—*Judith R. Robinson*

What Joy There Was

Young or old, skin serves:
borders keep innards in place.
Young or old, we believe wings
encompass universal detritus:
car keys, single socks, diamonds,
Erno's cracked limbs,
his woman's fat hips,
her mother's sagging knees,
the dogwood's budding branches.
We believe all is counted.
Yet Erno's gang is not much involved—
it goes on with or without them.

The waters ripple and flow with fish
and even if reproduction slows in Europe,
it does not halt. Therefore
the gang chooses hard
to remember what joy there was
in Miami, the Christmas of '68,
they watched, with their little boy, the
plastic pine tree change
from bright red to white to cobalt blue
then, at once, to all the glory colors.

—Judith R. Robinson

Pittsburgh, 1985

H. saw a rat
In the back
Of Rosenbloom's Bakery
Where she worked
The summer she was fifteen.
It was gray and huge
And the first of its kind
She ever met.
Naturally she screamed
And dropped a tray
Of fresh baked kichel.
Also working at the bakery
was an extremely old countess
Way down on her luck
Here in America.

Among the family stories
We tell we mention
This as the summer
Of the rat and the countess.
An adventure from
The bright green time
of becoming for H
which certainly
seemed a beginning
but like all starts are
false and lead
down ways that
smoothly rise
and unexpectedly fall
but always end.

—*Judith R. Robinson*

Hate

was the word gruelingly put together
by the automaton using "baby blocks" like sutures.

Found objects are his only way to speak,
along with a few clunky hand signals which squeak.

He has trouble moving his clockworks and gears.
They have corroded from all his tears.

The alley way behind the scrap yard is his home.
He searches for spare parts, but finds none. He wants chrome.

Two friends—a pigeon named Kurt, and a rat named Renaldo
pick at his fading eyes and nibble at his twisted toes.

Wait! Watch. Now, he is spelling another word.

H...E...L...P.

—Nick Romeo

Strange How Things Happen

My sentences sometimes end
with a silly little giggle
like my mother's used to do.

My mother read Thoreau,
her dictionary handy,
When I take my favorite composing chair
I always keep Webster,
Shipley and Roget
very close.

My mother had a house rule: Never
interrupt someone who is singing
and she sang lovesongs while she did housework.
I sang lovesongs
and folksongs and ballads and hymns.

So I ate my mother.
Swallowed her whole.
I don't remember how or when
but I must have tipped my head *way*
back—I saw Popeye's Olive Oyl,
hands clasped, blissful upturned eyes,
head surrounded with little red cartoon hearts—
and I lowered her long, stretched-out form
into my gaping mouth and
she slithered down my gullet.
And stayed there.

—Lucille T. Seibert

The Small Calculator

I held in my hand a small calculator
and wondered, if I pressed it three times
what would happen.
So three times I pressed it
and three times it beeped
and suddenly I knew I had summoned
the E.M.T. I knew
what I had done was wrong. I stood waiting
just inside the front door
cradling my arms, wanting to hold my cat
who was in the living room asleep.
I heard the sirens. They couldn't
have my cat. I wouldn't let them
have my cat...

They say first thought on waking
is part of the dream.
I lay one hour on my bed,
numbers games in my mind.
The answer was always nine
or multiples of nine. The philosopher.
I am waiting to be taken
wounded from the battlefield.

—*Lucille T. Seibert*

There's a Person Inside My Computer

I sit before the lighted screen
and this note
flashes before my eye.

"I will no longer check
your spelling and punctuation;
you make too many mistakes."

I thought these corrections were automatic.
You know—a misspelled word
triggers a squiggly line.
But hey, there's a real live person
inside this thing.

I check:
All the wires are plugged in.
Where is he, anyhow?

Oh, I think I see him...

A balding man in his tiny office—
shirt-sleeves pushed up,
wearing suspenders
and a cap with translucent green visor.
Drinks lots of black coffee.
Mutters under his breath.
He's shuffling papers—hey, that's my poem!
He's lighting a match to my poem!

—Lucille T. Seibert

To Sleep

I lie on my bed, returning
to sleep, that beautiful garden of peace.

"Fall in love with your world
all over again and take care of you,
don't get old," I tell everyone.

I hear the ticking of the bedside clock,
the constant ringing in my left ear
and the raindrops on the porch roof.

All day my left ear rings;
it seems louder at night.

I rest on a billowy cloud of music...
the clock, the ringing in my ear, the rain...

The man in the house next to mine put a tent
on his roof. In the spring he will paint
a mural on the side wall of his house.

If I had a side wall, I would paint
a mural of those French dancing girls.

—*Lucille T. Seibert*

Working on the Old House

Gone almost three years,
I still keep my tools
apart from his tools.

—*John Stokes*

Cabin

What is the story
of the fallen down shack
the size of a two car garage

Two walls down, one leaning, one upright
with a single door bolted shut,
on the inside

—John Stokes

Young Mexican Couple

kissing
on the stairwell
with intensity
I envy

for all I know
they aren't even legally
here
though their libidos
certainly aren't
elsewhere
I wish
I could say the same

they are obeying
laws of nature
which precede
those of state
in the broader scheme
I may be the one
who's disobeyed
her grace,
whose soul

has already
been deported.

—Christine Telfer

Death (Смерть)

for Alla

It's not that I miss her the way one
misses a lover—or even a close friend
or family member, for that matter.

There is no aching hole in my heart that
drips out thoughts of her, no old familiar
pang in my guts where they must land,

burning, no unsettling absences
suggested by an empty chair, or voice
oddly missing from the conversation.

This was a woman I hadn't seen in years.

I promised I would visit but I didn't.
And then she moved. Again.
I never made it to the new apartment.

Next thing you know, I heard
she was living in a nursing home.
Was I surprised? After all, *Alla's old.*

I resolved to visit. Someday. Soon.
I didn't realize how soon it would have it be.

I imagined our visit in my mind
as if we'd had it, could almost hear
our words as if we'd said them.

I'd practice a few words of my meager
Russian on her, *"Kak da la?"* 'Harasho,
a vy?'. And she would ramble on

in phrases well beyond my grasp, no idea
I wasn't comprehending until the long
silence

following a question posed repeatedly.
"ne paniymaete?" '*ney.*' It would be a few minutes
before she'd understand that I didn't understand.

And then we'd talk about the books.
I'd return her copy of Pushkin's *Eugene Onegin,*
(which I never finished, by the way)

and she'd give back the tattered paperback
of Mandelstam's poems I'd loaned her in exchange.
I can still see the cover of that one, though the image
is almost as faded in my in my memory as the graying

thing was in print.
I'll never see that book again.
And I barely remember the poems.

I can see the faded black and white cover,
fading, can see language, poetry
and knowledge fading,

An alphabet I once knew,
fading

can see Alla,
a whole generation of Russians, fading
Something I meant to say, something I meant to do...

another generation of Russians
fading

I never got around to visiting Alla
as she lay dying in a nursing home.
Had more pressing things to do.

I never mastered Russian, either.
And sometimes I fear I have forgotten
half of what I once knew.

—*Christine Telfer*

My Husband Buys Cheese at Pennsylvania Macaroni Co.

My favorite's semi-soft, split by a layer of ash.
Not mold. Melting indulgence, penance, melting again.
At our wedding he smashed
a flash bulb in place of the traditional glass
while uncles shouted encouragements, traditionally crass.

Even the name, Morbier, smacks of death.
Maybe it's Basque.
The aisle that leads to the altar is lined with *crash*.
Volcanic soils are fertile, so after eruptions
people repeople the slippery scree.

Weddings were about repeopling then,
the community-approved means of production.
Kauai was paradise though damaged by Iniki.
An old discursive cookbook says, *What a friend
we have in cheeses.*

I think we'll go together to the end.
Morbier is edible, even to the rind.

—*Arlene Weiner*

Flamenco Dancer in White

Oh, my girl, city bird, when I see you stand
above the others, head high, skirts high,
I believe you're beautiful. You're ready
to stamp your heels, swirl, leaving behind
the gray day, when you peck peck peck,
head down, on the gray street for bread.
You're not pretty, city bird, you're like me, pure
as city snow. Now spine straight, neck long,
for a minute you belong above the others.
Stretch upward, assured—fly.
City bird, dance for us, who keep our heads low,
dance more furiously than falling city snow.

—Arlene Weiner

113

Like Love

Once, on a woodland path, you saw a toad
and pointed it out to the children. They shouted,
Catch it! Catch it! You tried, but were empty handed,
covered the place in the road
           where it had been.

Then I, not quick of hand or eye—
who'd never pounded fist into mitt, waiting
to make a game-saving quick stop
or breathtaking stretch and reach,
                I got it!—

stepped up and covered it on my first try.
That was a lesson. To catch
the slow, large, warty, skeptical thing
you have to want
           to catch it,

be willing
        to hold it.

—*Arlene Weiner*

Cirque de Lune
—for Michael Wurster

You take me to a circus in the dark,
buy me candy and a fake
snake. I'm a child.

I hear the slap of blind
trapeze artists making catches.
An odor of elephant then
or drunk men waltzing in leather.

When they announce the knife thrower
and his beautiful wife
I feel something slide
quick quick cold cold against my side.

Best of all, the calliope.
Faint, grateful. I hold my breath,
it stops.

At the last,
for the recessional,
a clown plays guitar in Spanish

and one white light, high,
round, pale, comes on
and the audience
is illuminated.

—*Arlene Weiner*

115

If You Went Away

If you went away it would be like winter—
like Times Square, midnight,
New Year's Eve.
I'd get used to drinking
the whole pot of coffee
if you'd ever leave.

I'd sleep in the middle of the bed until late.
If you left me I'd miss you
because I can't throw straight.

If you left I'd be
like a horse out of water,
a prisoner without a cell
or a jailor.
I'd get the right kind of yogurt.
I'd eat organic lettuce.
It'd really be hell
o sailor!

Because how do I need you?
Like a hole in the head
like a hole in the shoe
like a hole in the hat
that I'm talking through.

—*Arlene Weiner*

Lamentation

By the great river that flows two ways
I met him. Then I was a yellow boat
for the wreathed king. During the longest days
in that flat country we rowed
among reed birds to the border of the sea.

At the border of the sea, painted with sun, I thirsted.
We drank each other at the river mouth.
Salt, fresh. He was whole then, his thighs
a branched tree. Now I burst
with salt pain like a shad in spring.

Winter after winter he has lain with my rival.
He has wreathed his head with her heavy gray crown.
She has clasped him between her icy thighs, and strewn
his members along the rivers. Shad, where did you travel?
Bitterns, where were you? Why did you not cry out?

Spring after spring along the rivers
I have searched for his scattered parts,
gathered them, stitched them together
with song. I have sung with a drying throat.
This spring, this spring, I cannot find his heart.

I will cry out for the long days, the sun,
the green wreath. I will swim to the fresh water,
deliver myself of salt. Oh, my black opponent,
will you give me your lead shoes, will I lie down with you,
can I love you, since you have won, my beautiful one?

—Arlene Weiner

Comfort Zone

They come after work
through sugar-white snow falling
pink under anti-crime lights, sit

in this room under water.
They keep it light, laugh while he floats
over their talk like the fluorescent fixture.

A capable man on a ladder
last Saturday fixing a basement light
when his wife heard…

she turns from the memory, returns, returns.
He lay on the cellar floor, out like—
shattered. In induced coma now,

damaged. He hovers, their hopes hover,
in the shadowless light of the family
waiting room.

Whether his light is quite out, whether
his hands will grasp, move, whether
he'll return with speech, memory—fixed—

how much? they don't ask. *He's
in capable hands, they say, Hey, leave
some of that pizza*, step out to light cigarettes,

tell stories smoothed like rosary beads—
*Remember the time the lights went out
during the Super Bowl?* that show him
in a good light. Absurd. Furious. Whole.

—*Arlene Weiner*

A Craft
—For my mother

Vermeer's lacemaker's hands,
as she bends to her bobbin,
are blessed by a milky light,

but your knuckles dance,
complicating a string,
in mere air, mirrored

in windows of permanent night.
The subway roars and screeches.
Turned toward somebody's talk

your face takes no notice
as your fingers row
autonomous, knotting a net.

A hook rocks in your right hand,
catches a twist from the left, and grows
an endless coil, a snail,

saucer, bowl, almost a globe.
And caught in it will flash
sequins like dimes, silver night fish.

You are making a hat for Othello's head
or Crystal's. It will cradle the skull.
Your web will keep them warm

in a New York winter.
The knack of this, the skill.
Simple. The keeping at it.

—*Arlene Weiner*

The Hotel Earle

Correpondences.

Tom Russell in a concert
at Pittsburgh Center for the Arts
mentions the Hotel Earle in Greenwich Village,
a cheap place for musicians to stay
"back in the day."

Then, in Lisa Jarnot's biography of Robert Duncan,
she mentions Duncan stayed at the Hotle Earle
in April 1962 on one of his visits to New York City.

Correspondences.

What do you do
if you're two white girls
and a black guy,
Judy Jones, Sue Rehr and Lenny King,
it's 1962
and you've just met in New York City
and you're in bed together at the Hotel Earle,
what do you do?

Why, you phone Michael
back in Carlisle, 2:00 a.m.,
to share the joy.

Correspondences.

The Hotel Earle became a welfare hotel
and burned down.
Bob Nelson's father lived there.
He was murdered
in 1971
in Central Park.

I remember a nearby mission.
They had soup and doughnuts.
You had to listen to the sermon first.

—*Michael Wurster*

123

Outpost

Push pins arrayed on the map—
blue, red, yellow, green,
some black along the coastline.

Debris from the ceiling
falls into my coffee.

The weather keeps us inside.
It makes the TV pictures snowy.

Some of the rooms are empty and unheated.

They call me the fisherman.

—Michael Wurster

Imagination

for Suzanne

From the balcony of the rented vacation apartment
the two of you share in northern Arkansas,
Horseshoe Bend, you
look down to the lake in the moonlight

where two men are in the water,
skinny-dipping,
one your poet lover,
the other, Benedict, the current pope.

This is the magic of it.
He can call on the great or humble,
the real or fanciful, living
or dead, to his side in the moonlight

for your astonishment. Just two older men
enjoying the water on a summer's night.

—*Michael Wurster*

In Suzanne's House

Everywhere one looks
there is a treat,

a painting of red poppies
in a vase,

a pewter tea service.

—*Michael Wurster*

Afterword

We hope you have enjoyed reading the poems of the members of The Pittsburgh Poetry Exchange. There are many people to thank for the creation of this anthology, first being RD Armstrong, publisher, LUMMOX Press. RD is a kindred poetic spirit, one who found us, and without whose support and encouragement this book would not have happened.

We are grateful to our wonderful city, a lively home for art and artists. Pittsburgh has long been a hub of happenings. With its beautiful topography of hills and rivers, its interesting history as well as its unique ethnic mix of people, Pittsburgh itself continues to offer so much that nurtures us.

A thank you goes to the Brentwood Library, our gracious hosts, and to Barry Govenor who serves on the Library's board of directors and is one of our group. The library furnishes us with comfortable space, tables, chairs and coffee; every comfort to support our insatiable habit of meeting each month to workshop poetry.

We of the Pittsburgh Poetry Exchange are grateful to our founder, Michael Wurster, for his many years of mentoring every one of us. We have benefited more than can ever be expressed from his expertise, his guidance and his loyalty to poetry and to us.

Finally, I personally wish to thank my fellow workshoppers for their unending humor, friendship and always fine-tuned opinions. We have all enjoyed many years of listening, sharpening skills and advising one another on the countless aspects of our shared passion, poetry. Thanks, Guys!

—*Judith R. Robinson*

Contributors

Michael Albright has published poems in *Loyalhanna Review, Uppagus, U.S. 1Worksheets, The New People, the Pittsburgh Post-Gazette,* among other journals; he has work upcoming in *Stray Branch* and *Wilderness House Review.* He lives on a windy hilltop in Greensburg, PA, with his wife Lori and an ever-changing array of children and other animals.

Joan E. Bauer is the author of *The Almost Sound of Drowning*, Main Street Rag, 2008. Her poetry has appeared in numerous journals including *5 AM, Pearl, Poet Lore, Quarterly West, Slipstream,* and *U.S. 1 Worksheets,* and in over a dozen anthologies, among them, *Along These Rivers: Poetry and Photography from Pittsburgh* Quadrant, 2008, *Come Together: Imagine Peace,* Bottom Dog Press, 2008, and Only *the Sea Keeps: Poetry of the Tsunami,* Rupa & Co and Bayeux Arts, 2005, which she co edited with Judith R. Robinson and Sankar Roy. In 2007, her poem "Sleepers," won the Earle Birney Poetry Prize from *Prism International.* For some years, Joan worked as a teacher and counselor and now divides her time between Venice, CA and Pittsburgh, PA where she co-hosts and curates the Hemingway's Summer Poetry Series with Jimmy Cvetic. Her second book of poetry, *Glass Blocks & Begonias,* is forthcoming from Tebot Bach.

Jennifer Jackson Berry is the author of chapbooks *When I Was a Girl*, 2014, Sundress Publications and *Nothing But Candy,* 2003, Liquid Paper Press. A Pushcart Prize nominee, her recent poems have appeared in *Harpur Palate,* Green *Mountain Review, Connotation Press,* and *Cider Press,* among others. She holds degrees from the University of Pittsburgh and Indiana University's MFA program. She is a poetry reader for *WomenArtsQuarterly Journal.*

Ziggy Edwards' poems and short stories have appeared publications such as *5 AM, Confluence, Main Street Rag*, the *Pittsburgh Post-Gazette*, and *Ship of Fools.* Her chapbook, *Hope's White Shoes*, Pittsburgh Poetry Exchange, was published in 2006. With her son Jude she co-founded an online magazine, *Uppagus.*

Timons Esaias is a satirist, poet, essayist and writer of short fiction, living in Pittsburgh. His works have appeared in sixteen languages. He has been a finalist for the British Science Fiction Award, and won the 2005 Asimov's Readers Award for poetry. His story "Norbert and the System" has appeared in a textbook, and in college curricula. Literary publications include *5 AM, Connecticut Review* and *Barbaric Yawp.* He teaches in Seton Hill's Writing Popular Fiction MFA Program.

Mark Goldman was born in Philadelphia and has lived in Pittsburgh for 41 years. He is employed in the horticulture industry as a manufacturer's representative and consultant. He has been writing for many years. These are his first published poems.

Barry Govenor, B.A., CNMT, CRCST, is a retired healthcare worker who lives with his wife and two dogs in Brentwood, PA. His poetry has been published in *The Pittsburgh Post-Gazette, The Pittsburgh Quarterly, Flipside, The Loyalhanna Review* and other small presses. He has led workshops at the Bentwood Public Library, where he serves as a member of the Board of Trustees.

Johnny Hartner is a native of Pittsburgh. A graduate of Carnegie Mellon University and Duquesne University, he is a full-time professor of English at Community College of Allegheny County. His work has appeared in *Illya's Honey, Krax, Gargoyle, Poetry Motel.*

Gene Hirsch is an academic geriatrician who, for many years, has taught human values and the emotional care of sick and dying people to medical students and doctors. He has conducted poetry workshops widely for health professionals as an expressive adjunct to their caring experiences, as well as for poets in Western NC. He initiated a writing program at the John C. Campbell Folk School and has taught there for 22 years. His poetry has appeared in medical and non-medical journals such as *Pharos* (Medical Honor Society), *Hiram Poetry Review, Journal of Medical Humanities, Fetishes* (Univ. of

131

Colorado), and *The Journal of the American Medical Society.* He has written two books, *Along the Rutty Pot Hole Road* and *You Shall Die Again No More.* Anthologies include *Echoes Across the Blue Ridge, Tyranny of the Normal, Crossing Limits:African Americans and American Jews.* He has produced five volumes of *Freeing Jonah*, poetry from Western North Carolina.

Joe Kaldon lives in Aliquippa, PA. A graduate of Penn State University, he works as a product manager for a steel company. His poetry has been published in *Taproot Literary Review, Eye Contact, The Pittsburgh Post-Gazette* and the blog *99 Poems for the 99 Percent.* His chapbook, *Rust Belt,* is available at his website, *www.joekaldon.net.*

Sheila Kelly writes plays and poems. She is a member of The Madwomen in the Attic workshop, and a facilitator for The Pittsburgh Writer's Studio. Three of her plays received staged readings at the 2009 Pittsburgh Three Rivers Arts Festival. Her most recent work appears in *Brief Encounters:Ekphrases* from *the Spinning Plate Gallery,* the anthology *Voices from the Attic: Volume XIX* and in *Baily's Beads 2014,* where her poem, *The Frame,* was a poetry contest finalist.

Kathy McGregor grew up in a rural Western Pennsylvania town, left for the bigger world, settled in Pittsburgh long ago enough to qualify as an 'almost native.' She has worked as an English teacher, union organizer, non-profit director, social change advocate, and head of her own business. She currently owns and operates a specialty native plant nursery in Pittsburgh. Several of her poems appeared in *Mill Hunk Herald.* She is a regular in the Carnegie Mellon poetry class.

Yolanta Konewka Minor is a poet born in Poznan, Poland, living in Pittsburgh since 1982. Her education and experience is in the field of interior design. She was educated at The Art Institute of Pittsburgh and Point Park University. She is also a U.S. Certified Holistic Reflexologist. Jolanta has written poetry all her life. She is also a visual artist working in oils, oil pastel, and pencil. She is a practitioner of yoga and a member of One Pine Zen Meditation Sangha in Pittsburgh. These are her first published poems.

Edward Murray is the author of Stranger's Pilgrimage, published in *Dionne's Story*. He is past president and member of the Langston Hughes Poetry Society of Pittsburgh, and a member of the Pittsburgh Writer's Studio. Besides writing poetry, he is an artist, filmmaker and photographer whose work can be seen at *www.elmurray.com* and at the Braddock Carnegie Library.

Nick Romeo says: I am self-taught, and always strive to learn from my environment. Then I incorporate the multitude of subject matter into my artwork. My main forms of expression are 3D digital renderings, music, fractal generations, photography, sculpture and audio/video installation. And of course, poetry. I have displayed art at various galleries and other venues in the Pittsburgh area.

Stephen Pusateri lives in the South Hills area of Pittsburgh and works at WYEP-FM on its soul and blues programs. He studied English at the University of Pittsburgh and is actively involved in Pittsburgh's Bhutanese refugee community.

Judith R. Robinson is author of three poetry collections, the latest *Orange Fire*, Main Street Rag Publishing, 2012; a fiction collection, *The Beautiful Wife and Other Stories*, Aegina Press, 1996. She is editor or co-editor of ten poetry collections, the latest *The Poetry of Margaret Menamin*, three volumes, Main Street Rag Publishing, 2010, 2011,2012. She has received six awards for poetry writing and/or editing, the latest The Writer's Place (TWP) National Poetry Competition Award, 2012-2013 for her poem, "Urbanity". She teaches poetry at Osher/Carnegie Mellon University and Osher / University of Pittsburgh.

Lucille T. Seibert was born in New York, NY, lived in Boston, Mass, and moved to Pittsburgh in 1974. She attended Northeastern University, Marlboro College and Harvard University, and is an honors graduate of Community College of Allegheny County with a degree in Art. Her book, *The Unattended Kitchen Sink* was published by Claassen-Langer Publishing in 2011. Her poems have appeared in *Cafe Magazine, The Critic,* and *5AM*. She lives on a steep hill in Pittsburgh with her cat, Winston.

133

John Stokes is a retired medical technologist who lives in Pittsburgh. A member of Pittsburgh Poetry Exchange since 2006, he works mostly in the short form.

Christine Telfer edited and published a small magazine, *The Exchange,* connected to, and named for The Pittsburgh Poetry Exchange in the 1990's. She currently teaches English as a Second Language as part of A.I.U.'s adult ESL program, which keeps her busy, though she still comes to Pittsburgh Poetry Exchange workshops whenever she can. Her poems have appeared in some 20 odd publications, including *Along These Rivers: Poetry& Photography from Pittsburgh, Main Street Rag, Whiskey Island, Rain City Review,* and *The Pittsburgh Post-Gazette.*

Arlene Weiner is the author of the poetry collection *Escape Velocity*, Ragged Sky, 2006, of which poet Joy Katz wrote, "I want to keep my favorite of these beautifully alert, surprising poems with me as I grow old." A MacDowell Colony fellow in 2008, Arlene has been a Shakespeare scholar, a cardiology technician, a college instructor, an editor, and a research associate in educational applications of cognitive science. Her poetry has been published in journals including *Off the Coast, Pleiades, Poet Lore,* and *U.S. 1 Worksheets,* anthologized, and read by Garrison Keillor on his *Writer's Almanac.* She contributes brief essays to Autumn House's *Coal Hill Review.* She maintains the web site for Pittsburgh Poetry Exchange.

Michael Wurster is a founding member of Pittsburgh Poetry Exchange. He lives on the South Side with his pal Hawthorne, a Siamese cat. Many credits and honors. His most recent book of poems is *The British Detective*, Main Street Rag Publishing, 2009.

ABOUT THE LUMMOX PRESS

LUMMOX Press was created in 1994 by **RD Armstrong**. It began as a self-publishing/ DIY imprint for poetry by RD, aka Raindog. Several chapbooks were published and in late 1995 LUMMOX began publishing the *LUMMOX Journal*, a monthly small/underground press lit-arts mag. Available primarily by subscription, the *LJ* continued its exploration of the "creative process" until its demise as a print mag in 2006. It was hailed as one of the best monthlies in the small press by John Berbrich and Todd Moore.

In 1998, LUMMOX began publishing the Little Red Book series, and continues to do so, sporadically, today. To date there are some 60 titles in the series and a collection of poems from the first decade of the series has been published under the title **The Long Way Home** (2009). It's a great way to explore the series.

Together with Chris Yeseta (layout and art direction since 1997), RD continues to publish books that are both striking in their looks as well as their content…*published because of the merit of the work, not the fame of the author*. That's why there are so many first full-length collections in the roster (look for the *).

* * *

The following books are available directly from the LUMMOX Press via its website: *www.lummoxpress.com/lc/* or at LUMMOX c/o PO Box 5301, San Pedro, CA 90733. There are also E-Copy (PDF) versions of most titles available. Books with the letters SPD are also carried by Small Press Distribution.

The Wren Notebook by Rick Smith (2000)
Last Call: The Legacy of Charles Bukowski edited by RD Armstrong (2004)
On/Off the Beaten Path by RD Armstrong (2008)
Fire and Rain—Selected Poems 1993-2007, Volumes 1 & 2 by RD Armstrong (2008)*
El Pagano and Other Twisted Tales by RD Armstrong (short stories—2008)*
New and Selected Poems by John Yamrus (2009)
The Riddle of the Wooden Gun by Todd Moore (2009)
Sea Trails by Pris Campbell (2009)

Down This Crooked Road—Modern Poetry from the Road Less Traveled edited by RD Armstrong and William Taylor, Jr. (2009)

Drive By by John Bennett (2010)

Modest Aspirations by Gerald Locklin & Beth Wilson (2010)

Steel Valley by Michael Adams (2010)*

Hard Landing by Rick Smith (2010)

A Love Letter to Darwin by Jane Crown (2010)*

E/OR—Living Amongst the Mangled by RD Armstrong (2010)

Ginger, Lily & Sweet Fire by H. Lamar Thomas (2010)*

Whose Cries Are Not Music by Linda Benninghoff (2011)*

Dog Whistle Politics by Michael Paul (2011)*

What Looks Like an Elephant by Edward Nudleman (2011)* SPD

Working the Wreckage of the American Poem edited by RD Armstrong (2011)

Living Among the Mangled (revised) by RD Armstrong, special edition, (2011)

The Accidental Navigator by Henry Denander (2011)

Catalina by Laurie Soriano (2011)* SPD

Born to Be Blue by Tony Moffeit (2011)

Last Call: the Bukowski Legacy Continues edited by RD Armstrong (2011)

Strong As Silk by Brigit Truex (2012)* SPD

The Instrument of Others by Leonard J. Cirino (2012)

If It We by Lisa Zaran (2012)*

The Names of Lost Things by Jason Hardung (2012)

Because, Just Because by Philip Ramp (2012)

Crazy Bone by Billy Jones (2012)

LUMMOX #1 edited by RD Armstrong (see description below—2012)

5150—A Memoir by Dana Christensen (2013)*

I See Hunger's Children by normal (2013)*

her by j/j hastain (2013)*
How Long the Night Is by Christine DeSimone (2013)
Songs of the Glue Machines by Nicholas Belardes (2013)
Breaking and Entering by D. R. Wagner (2013)
Me First by Ann Curran (2013)
What the Wind Says by Taylor Graham (2013)
Birth Mother Mercy by Alex Frankel (2013)
Broken Lines—The Art & Craft of Poetry by Judith Skillman (2013)
Walking the Puppy by Taylor Graham (2013)
Veritas Cabaret by Mende Smith(2013)
LUMMOX #2 edited by RD Armstrong (2013)
Whispering in a Mad Dog's Ear by Rick Smith (2014)
The Liberal Media Made Me Do It! edited by Robbi Nester (2014)
Unchainable Spirit edited by RD Armstrong (2014)
Ding Dong the Bell Pussy in the Well by Linda Lerner (2014)
Wildwood by Kyle Laws (2014)
Corvidae by B.J.Buckley (2014)
The Brentwood Anthology edited by Judith R. Robinson and Michael Wurster (2014)
A Tree on the Rift by Bruce Colbert (2014)*
LUMMOX #3 edited by RD Armstrong (2014)

* * *

LUMMOX (the anthology) is a yearly print anthology (begun in 2012). It contains interviews, essays, articles, reviews, artwork, ads and lots of poetry (future issues will also feature special flashbacks to the old *LUMMOX Journal* archives). The focus of the first issue was "Favorite Poems", the theme for #2 was PLACE and for the third issue: DESIRE / ROAD KILL. Each issue features poetry from around the world.

LUMMOX is available by annual subscription for $25 USA and $35 WORLD. Visit *http://www.lummoxpress.com/lc/lummox-anthology-2/* for details.